Relationship Builders

Ages 8-12

Relationship Builders

by
Joy Wilt
Bill Watson

Ages 8-12

EDUCATIONAL PRODUCTS DIVISION

Waco, Texas

To
Mitzi and Matthew Watson
and All the Other Children in the World Who Will, We Hope, Develop
Positive Relationships with Other Children

ACKNOWLEDGMENTS

We would like to thank Terre Watson, Robert C. Harrison, and Mary Donnelly for their research and for writing many of these creative relationship builders.

Our deep appreciation also goes to Rosanne Crist, who typed the original manuscript, Connie Vandenberg and Pat Pratt, Editors; Christina Kierman, Design Editor; and Jack Woodward, who developed the photographs.

CONTENTS

INTRODUCTION

Competition is healthy and good for all individuals. Competition provides growth potential, for it presents a challenge that can be met in a short amount of time. In other words, the results are known right away, and the results are what relationship builders are all about. Competition should be fun and should involve all the participants all the time. When winning becomes one's prime objective, then competition begins to present problems. One begins to see violence, injuries, neurotic behavior, and emotional conflicts, and negative relationships develop. Professional athletes have been, are, and always will be models that most children respect and admire. Every day professional athletics becomes more violent, more win-oriented, and less rule-conscious. This type of competition affects children. How many times do we ask our children: Well, did you win? How did you do? What did you win? How many points did you score? How many hits did you have? Did you win? Why not ask these questions: Did you have fun? Did you learn anything? Did you help anyone? Did you meet any new boys or girls? Do you want to go back?

The purpose of this book is to introduce many varied activities that are competition oriented but emphasize cooperation, being part of a team, fun, and trust. In these activities, competition is used to build self-confidence, self-awareness, and mutual trust. Rules can be adjusted to make the games more fun and the goals easier to obtain. When conducting an activity, don't hesitate to make variations. Sometimes the changes will work; sometimes they won't. But often the variations that do not work become the most fun. Also let the children make some variations; after all, they are the ones playing. Try to stay away from scorekeeping, winning, and losing. Remember: The people participating in the activity are much more important than the activity.

GAMES

1

UN-SCRAMBLE

SUGGESTED NUMBER: 8 or more

MATERIALS AND SUPPLIES: None

PROCEDURE

1. Stand in a small, tight circle.
2. Form a knot by holding on to the hands of 2 other people.
3. Do not hold on to the hand of the person next to you.
4. It will probably take a few minutes of switching hands before the knot is tied.
5. Without letting go of hands, untie the knot and form a circle. Pivoting on your handholds is permitted.

SQUAT WALK

SUGGESTED NUMBER: 10 or more

MATERIALS AND SUPPLIES: None

PROCEDURE

1. Form 2 lines, each child standing back-to-back with another.
2. One line stands still while the other line takes 1 step to the side in the same direction.
3. Everyone bends down, crosses arms, reaches through his or her legs, and grabs the hands of 2 individuals in the other line.
4. After everyone has done this, the group begins to walk.

VARIATION

Form 2 groups and use this activity as a relay.

LOG ROLL

MATERIALS AND SUPPLIES: None

PROCEDURE

1. Ask the children to lie down flat on their stomachs, as close to one another as possible. Heads should be all in the same direction.
2. Beginning at one end, the first child rolls over all the other individuals.
3. After the first child has rolled over 5 or 6 children, the next child begins.
4. As each child gets to the end, he or she lies as close to the end person as possible.
5. Make sure that the children keep their elbows up while they are rolling. Also be sure that those who are lying down lie flat.

VARIATION

Use the Log Roll as a relay.

PASS THE TRASH

MATERIALS AND SUPPLIES

1. 1 trash can
2. 1 bat (rolled up sheets of newspaper) for every 2 people
3. Numerous balls of newspaper

PROCEDURE

1. Divide the group into 2 teams.
2. Draw a circle 6 feet in diameter on the floor. Set the trash can in the middle.
3. Team 1 lies down around the can with their heads against the can. Equip each team member with a bat.
4. Team 2 stands around the circle. Each team member is equipped with balls of newspaper.
5. Team 2 attempts to throw the paper into the can.
6. Team 1 tries to prevent the balls from going into the can by batting the balls away with their bats.
7. After a determined time (2 minutes or so) play is halted. The leader then counts the balls in the can.
8. Teams then switch positions, and the game is played again.

SIT-IN

SUGGESTED NUMBER: 25 or more

MATERIALS AND SUPPLIES: None

PROCEDURE

1. Form a circle and have everyone move as close to one another as possible.
2. Everyone turns and faces the same direction and moves as close to one another as possible.
3. All persons put their hands on the waist of the person in front of them.
4. Very slowly and at the same time, all persons sit on the knees of the person behind them.
5. Hint: Don't try to accomplish the entire activity the first time. Have all persons bend their knees and begin to sit down without losing their balance. Then have everyone stand up and gradually try again.

ADD AN ACTION

SUGGESTED NUMBER: 2 or more

MATERIALS AND SUPPLIES: None

PROCEDURE

1. The group forms a circle, and 1 person is picked to initiate an action (for example, tapping head or knee). All members mimic the action.
2. The child on the first person's left then adds another action, and all players do both actions simultaneously.
3. The game continues until it is impossible to add any more actions.
4. It is best to keep the game moving quickly.

BACKUP

SUGGESTED NUMBER: 2 or any number of groups of 2

MATERIALS AND SUPPLIES: None

PROCEDURE

1. Ask each member of the group to find a partner.
2. Ask the couples to sit on the floor, back to back.
3. Have each couple interlock elbows.
4. Ask each couple to stand up together.
5. It sounds easy, but the couples will discover it takes a lot of cooperation and balance to stand up together.
6. Change partners so that everyone can have several turns.

ROUND TAG

SUGGESTED NUMBER: 10 to 100

MATERIALS AND SUPPLIES: Rope

PROCEDURE

1. Tie both ends of the rope in a knot to form a circle.
2. Place the rope on the ground.
3. Put half the group inside the circle and half the group outside the circle.
4. Both groups try to pull the rope toward their own side. The inside group pulls toward the center, and the outside group pulls toward the outside of the circle.

THREE IN A PAIR

SUGGESTED NUMBER: 3 or any number of groups of 3

MATERIALS AND SUPPLIES: Several large pairs of pants

PROCEDURE

1. Sew together the outside leg seams of 3 pairs of pants. The finished product should look like it would fit a 6-legged monster.
2. Put 3 children in the pants, and instruct them to walk to the opposite side of the room or yard.
3. Six-legged pants are great to use in relay races.

TUNNEL OF LOVE

SUGGESTED NUMBER: 20 or more

MATERIALS AND SUPPLIES: None

PROCEDURE

1. Darken the room, and ask all children to form a tight circle.
2. The children in the center are instructed to get on their hands and knees and crawl to the center of the group.
3. After the first children have gone, the children who are now in the center do likewise.
4. Continue until circle eventually breaks up.

BACK-SEAT DRIVERS

SUGGESTED NUMBER: 6 or more

MATERIALS AND SUPPLIES: None

PROCEDURE

1. Blindfold 2 children and ask them to form a seat by grasping each other's wrists.
2. Another child then sits on the seat and becomes the driver.
3. Without speaking, the driver leads the blindfolded pair in and out of obstacles.
4. This game can be played as a group effort, competing against the clock, or as a relay.

PING-PONG BLOW

SUGGESTED NUMBER: 8 or more

MATERIALS AND SUPPLIES

1. Large table
2. Ping-Pong ball

PROCEDURE

1. Gather the children around a table that has a line dividing it in half.
2. Set a Ping-Pong ball on the table.
3. All children attempt to blow the ball onto their opponents' side of the table.

TOOTHPICK HUNT

SUGGESTED NUMBER: 6 or more

MATERIALS AND SUPPLIES: A box of toothpicks

PROCEDURE

1. Divide the children into groups of 3.
2. One child is the hider, one the finder, and the third is the keeper.
3. The finder leaves the room; the hider hides toothpicks in the keeper's clothes and on his or her body.
4. The finder returns and has 1 minute to find as many toothpicks as possible.

HUMAN TICK-TACK-TOE

SUGGESTED NUMBER: 10 or more

MATERIALS AND SUPPLIES

A tick-tack-toe diagram marked off on the ground

PROCEDURE

1. Divide the children into 2 teams.
2. Designate 1 team as the x's, the other the o's.
3. Play tick-tack-toe with all members of a team agreeing on their team's move.
4. Once the team members agree on a move, they send 1 of their players to that particular square. This child is still involved in the decision making.
5. Play the game until 1 team has filled 3 squares in a row or until all squares are filled.

BALLOON BASKETBALL

SUGGESTED NUMBER: 8 or more

MATERIALS AND SUPPLIES

2 balloons, each a different color

PROCEDURE

1. Divide the children into 2 teams.
2. Place 2 sturdy chairs at each end of the room.
3. A player from each team stands on 1 of the chairs.
4. Give each team a balloon.
5. The purpose of the game is for the player standing on the chair to pop the opponent's balloon.
6. The players on the chairs must remain on the chairs at all times.
7. Balloons must be kept in the air at all times either by hitting or blowing, with no passing or holding the balloon.

VARIATION

Each team can have as many as 5 or 6 balloons in the game at one time.

SUCKER RACE

SUGGESTED NUMBER: 6 or more

MATERIALS AND SUPPLIES

1. Straws for all players
2. 8½- by 11-inch sheets of paper for each group

PROCEDURE

1. Give each child a straw and each group a piece of paper.
2. Determine a starting point and a finishing point.
3. Ask 2 or more players to pick up the paper by sucking through their straws. Hands or other parts of the body may not be used.
4. The more children doing this at one time, the better.
5. Play the game as a relay.

VARIATION

See how many pieces of paper each group can transfer from 1 point to another in a set amount of time.

TUG OF WAR

SUGGESTED NUMBER: 12 or more

MATERIALS AND SUPPLIES

A rope approximately 75 feet long and 2 inches thick.

PROCEDURE

1. Divide the group into 2 teams.
2. Lay the rope out in a straight line. Tie a flag in the center. Mark a line 15 feet to each side of the center.

3. Each team lines up in single file, facing each other along-side the rope.
4. On the command of "go," each team grasps the rope and tries to pull the other team toward their direction.
5. The game is over when the flag crosses one of the boundary lines.

VARIATION

In the middle of the game, as both teams are struggling, the leader yells "switch," and both teams drop the rope and run to the opposite side and proceed to pull again.

FOUR-WAY TUG OF WAR

SUGGESTED NUMBER: 40 or more

MATERIALS AND SUPPLIES

A rope approximately 100 feet long and 2 inches thick

PROCEDURE

---

1. Tie the ends of the rope together.
2. Form the rope into a large square on the ground.
3. Divide the children into 4 equal teams.
4. Each team stands to the outside of the rope so that as a group they also form a square.
5. On the command of "go," each team pulls the rope in its direction, attempting to reach an outside line 15 feet away.

EGG TOSS

MATERIALS AND SUPPLIES

1 raw egg per team

PROCEDURE

1. Divide the group into equal teams of 6 or more.
2. Each team forms a line and faces the other, approximately 9 feet apart.
3. The teams toss the egg back and forth until it breaks or until a certain time limit has been reached.
4. Have each team go one at a time, and see how many times the team members can successfully catch the egg during a set time-limit.

HUFF 'N PUFF

SUGGESTED NUMBER: 4 or more

MATERIALS AND SUPPLIES

1. Twine
2. Paper cups

PROCEDURE

1. Put a hole in the bottom of each cup.
2. Tie one end of the twine to a piece of sturdy furniture or a fixture. Thread the other end of the twine through the bottom of the cup and tie the twine to another piece of furniture or a fixture across the room. Make sure the cup slides easily along the twine.
3. Ask 2 or 3 players from each team to blow the cup from a starting point to a finish point and then push the cup back to the starting point.
4. This game can be used as a relay, or teams can compete against time.

CONTAGIOUS GAME

SUGGESTED NUMBER: 10 to 20

MATERIALS AND SUPPLIES: None

PROCEDURE

1. Ask the group to form a circle.
2. The first child initiates some kind of action (tapping head, jumping up and down, waving arms).
3. The second child must start with the first child's action and then begin an action of his or her own.

4. The third child repeats the actions of the first and second child and then starts one of his or her own.
5. This process continues around the circle until it reaches the first child again.
6. The first child must repeat all the actions.
7. Have the whole group participate to help each child remember the previous action.

BASKETBALL POP

SUGGESTED NUMBER: 8 or more

MATERIALS AND SUPPLIES

1. 2 full sheets of newspaper
2. Balloons
3. 2 straight pins
4. 2 chairs

PROCEDURE

1. Divide the children into 2 teams.
2. Tape the newspapers on 2 opposite walls, with the bottom edge of the newspaper about 4 feet from the floor.
3. Put the back of 1 chair against each wall directly under the newspaper.
4. Each team stands on the opposite side of the room and faces the goal.
5. Each team throws a balloon into the air and bats it toward the goal, trying to hit the newspaper.
6. Standing on the chairs, the goalies attempt to pop the other team's balloon with the straight pin.
7. Teams may not interfere with the other team's balloons.

BALLOON VOLLEYBALL

SUGGESTED NUMBER: 6 or more

MATERIALS AND SUPPLIES

1. Water balloon
2. Twine

PROCEDURE

1. Tie the twine to 2 objects approximately 6 feet from the ground.
2. Divide the children into 2 or more teams. Have each team form a straight line.
3. One child from each team tosses the water balloon over the twine and catches it.
4. Have each child go 2 times.
5. Award 5 points for each remaining balloon, 10 points for finishing first, 5 points for second, and 1 point for third.
6. This game can be used as a relay or the teams may compete against the clock.

WRIST PASS

SUGGESTED NUMBER: 10 or more

MATERIALS AND SUPPLIES: Beanbag or paper plate

PROCEDURE

1. Divide into 2 teams and form straight lines, facing each other.

2. Each player grasps the left wrist of the player on the right.
3. The object of the game is to pass the paper plate or bean-bag down the line.
4. If the object is dropped, the entire team must bend down to pick it up.
5. This game can be used as a relay or the teams may compete against the clock.

BODY FLOAT

SUGGESTED NUMBER: 20 or more

MATERIALS AND SUPPLIES: None

PROCEDURE

1. Ask the children to form 2 single-file lines, shoulder to shoulder.
2. Urge them to form a tight line.
3. The child at the front of each line leans back into the arms of the children behind him or her. The first child is then lifted overhead and passed to the rear of the line.
4. Tell the children to extend their arms and elbows.
5. The game continues until each child has an opportunity to float down the line.
6. One adult should supervise each group.

PYRAMIDS

SUGGESTED NUMBER: 6 or more

MATERIALS AND SUPPLIES: None

PROCEDURE

1. Have 3 children squat down as close together as possible.
2. Put 2 individuals on top of them.
3. Finish off the pyramid with 1 smaller individual on top.
4. The pyramids can go as high as the children like.
5. There is a great sense of accomplishment among the children when the pyramids are completed.
6. Always have a spotter.

DRAGON TAIL

SUGGESTED NUMBER: 10 or more

MATERIALS AND SUPPLIES: None

PROCEDURE

1. Form a single line with each child's arms wrapped tightly around the person in front of him or her.
2. The object of the game is for the person in the front to hook on to the person at the end of the line.
3. When the head of the dragon does catch the tail, the head becomes the tail, and the next person in line becomes the head.

VARIATION

Have 4 or 5 dragons going at one time, with the heads permitted to hook on to any tail.

OBJECT RELAY

SUGGESTED NUMBER: 12 or more

MATERIALS AND SUPPLIES

A table full of objects of different sizes

PROCEDURE

1. Divide the group into 2 teams (9 players would be the ideal team).
2. Each team forms squads of 3 players each.
3. On the leader's call of "go," the first squad from each team holds hands, runs to the table full of objects, and picks up an item. The rule is that all players must be touching the item.
4. The squad returns the item to their team and passes the item to the next squad. The second squad, holding the first item, runs to the table and obtains another item. They return and pass both items to the next squad.
5. The game ends when an object is dropped while being transported.

WET-HAND RELAY

SUGGESTED NUMBER: 12 or more

MATERIALS AND SUPPLIES

1. A bucket of water
2. 1 coffee can per team

36

1. Divide into 2 or more teams.
2. One member from each team takes off his or her shirt, lies down, and places a coffee can on his or her chest.
3. The other team members line up approximately 20 feet behind the bucket.
4. The goal is to fill the coffee can with water transported only by cupped hands.
5. On "go," the teams attempt to fill their coffee cans.
6. *Note:* The most successful teams will work together.
7. This game can be played as a total group effort against the clock or as a race between teams.

HOP A LONG

SUGGESTED NUMBER: 6 or more

MATERIALS AND SUPPLIES

1. Record player
2. Recordings of lively music

PROCEDURE

1. Ask the children to form a circle and join hands.
2. When the music starts, children hop on one foot.
3. When the music stops, children stand on one leg until the music starts again.

MAR-LOON GOLF

SUGGESTED NUMBER: 2 or more

MATERIALS AND SUPPLIES

1. A blown-up balloon with a marble inside ("golf ball") for each individual or team
2. Rolled-up sheets of newspaper ("clubs") for each individual
3. Cardboard box

PROCEDURE

1. If the group is large, divide into subgroups of 3 or 4 people per group.
2. Give each child a "club" and a "golf ball."
3. The object is to hit the balloon into the box with the fewest attempts.
4. The box is set at the opposite end of the room from the children.
5. The groups alternate and count the number of strokes required to get the balloon into the box.

TARP TOSS

SUGGESTED NUMBER: 20 or more

MATERIALS AND SUPPLIES

A large, strong canvas tarp

PROCEDURE

1. Space the group evenly around the tarp.
2. Ask for a volunteer to lie in the center of the tarp and be tossed into the air and caught.
3. Stress the importance of teamwork and the fact that everyone must hold on tightly for this activity to be successful.
4. After the volunteer lies in the center of the tarp, the group reaches down, takes hold of the tarp, and slowly raises it to waist level.
5. On the count of 3, the group raises the tarp and the person on it. The children then return the tarp to waist level, waiting to catch their friend.

SHAKE-A-RAKE RELAY

2 or more teams of 6 children each

MATERIALS AND SUPPLIES

1. One grass rake per team
2. 20 lightweight objects (for example, styrofoam balls, paper balls, and so on) per team

PROCEDURE

1. Divide the children into teams of 6 or more.
2. Three children from each team hold the rake while the rest of the team piles the 20 lightweight objects onto the rake.
3. At a designated starting sound, the trios take their rake and walk or run across the field, around a chair, and back to their team and hand the rake to the next 3 teammates.
4. The relay continues until every team member has run the course 5 times.
5. The goal is to move as quickly as possible without dropping any of the objects.
6. Award points for finishing first and for the number of objects left on the rake when finished.

SIMULATIONS

2

FRIENDS

SUGGESTED NUMBER: 1 or more

MATERIALS AND SUPPLIES

Paper and pencil for each child

PROCEDURE

1. Have each child make a list of 5 to 10 friends.
2. Under each friend's name, list the answers to the following questions:
   a. When did you meet?
   b. How did you meet?
   c. What do you like most about this person?
   d. What do you like least about this person?
   e. What do you enjoy doing most with this person?
   f. What is your friend's favorite TV program?
   g. What is your friend's favorite food?
   h. Where does your friend most enjoy going?
   i. What is your friend's middle name?
   j. What time does your friend have to go to bed at night?
   k. What color of eyes does your friend have?
3. Discuss the following questions in either small or large groups:
   a. Are you surprised at how much or how little you know about your friends?
   b. What makes a good friend?
   c. Is it necessary to know a lot about a person in order for that person to be a good friend?

FOR MY FRIEND I WOULD . . .

SUGGESTED NUMBER: 6 or more

MATERIALS AND SUPPLIES

1. Pencil and paper
2. List of questions for each group

PROCEDURE

1. Divide into groups of 3 to 6 children. Give each group a list of incomplete statements or read them aloud.
2. Children may answer the statements silently to themselves or write their answers on paper. Ask for volunteers to share their answers.
3. Allow group discussion and then go on to the next statement.
4. Suggested statements:
   a. If a friend forgot his or her lunch, I would . . .
   b. If my friend needed 25 cents, I would . . .
   c. If my friend wanted to copy my paper, I would . . .
   d. If my friend stole something and I knew it and someone asked me if my friend had taken it, I would . . .
   e. If I had only 1 cookie left and my friend walked up, I would . . .
   f. If my friend broke my favorite toy by accident, I would . . .
   g. If my friend promised to come over and then didn't, I would . . .

MY SECRETS

SUGGESTED NUMBER: 1 or more

MATERIALS AND SUPPLIES

Paper and pencil for each child

PROCEDURE

1. This simulation gives the participants the opportunity to discover the individuals with whom they are willing to share their secrets.
2. Make 5 columns with the following headings: self, parents, best friend, other friends, strangers.
3. Ask some of the following questions and have the participants put an "X" in the column that indicates with whom they would be willing to share their answer. They need not answer the questions, and they may check more than 1 column at a time.
   a. What are your pet likes and dislikes?
   b. When was the last time you cried? Why?
   c. Did you ever cheat at a game?
   d. Have you ever had a scary dream?
   e. Have you ever taken money from your mother or father without their permission?
   f. What activity or sport do you do the best?
   g. What is your favorite food?
   h. Were you ever cruel to an animal?
   i. Have you ever lied to your parents?

FINISH THE SENTENCE

MATERIALS AND SUPPLIES

Paper and pencil for each child

PROCEDURE

1. Read an unfinished sentence and ask the participants to write down their answers.
2. After all the questions have been completed, collect the papers and read some of the answers. The children do not put their names on the papers.
3. If the group is a close one, the children may want to answer the questions orally.
4. Suggested sentences:
   a. If I were president of the United States, I would . . .
   b. If I were 25 years old, I would . . .
   c. If I were of the opposite sex, I would . . .
   d. My favorite place is . . .
   e. I always laugh when . . .
   f. I wish I had . . .
   g. This weekend I wish I could go to . . .
   h. If I had 50 dollars I would . . .
   i. I'm afraid of . . .
   j. I cry when . . .
   k. If I were a teacher, I would . . .
   l. The worst thing a person can do is . . .
   m. The saddest day of my life was . . .

THAT'S ME— THAT'S NOT ME

SUGGESTED NUMBER: 1 or more

MATERIALS AND SUPPLIES

A list of choices for each person

PROCEDURE

1. Pass out the lists of choices or read the choices aloud and have each individual write down his or her answer.
2. Suggested choices: I see myself as . . .
   a. Blue or red
   b. Fast or slow
   c. Big or small
   d. A sports car or a camper
   e. A jet or a small private airplane
   f. An ocean or a lake
   g. Mickey Mouse or Donald Duck
   h. A road runner or a coyote
   i. President of the United States or mayor of a city
   j. A fireman or a policeman
   k. A tree or a flower
   l. An eagle or a hummingbird

THAT'S ME— THAT'S-NOT- ME COLLEC- TION

SUGGESTED NUMBER: 1 or more

MATERIALS AND SUPPLIES

2 shoe boxes for each child

PROCEDURE

1. This simulation works best after "That's Me—That's Not Me" has been used a few times.
2. Have each child decorate his or her box and identify one as "Me" and the other as "Not Me."
3. During the week, the children collect items that either relate to them or do not relate to them.
4. Let each child show his or her collections and explain the items.
5. If possible, save the boxes and allow the children to add or take away from them in succeeding weeks.

THE AUCTION

SUGGESTED NUMBER: 6 or more

MATERIALS AND SUPPLIES

1. A copy of the auction list for each group
2. 100 markers per group (to be used instead of money)

PROCEDURE

1. The purpose of this simulation is for the children to become aware of their priorities.
2. Divide into groups of 3 or 4.
3. Give each group 100 markers and a copy of the auction list.
4. Auction off each item on the list in the order of its appearance.
5. Children must bid as a group. When they run out of markers, they may no longer bid.
6. Some suggestions for an auction:

   a. All A's on a report card for 1 year
   b. Five hundred dollars for each member of the group
   c. An opportunity to be principal of their school for 2 weeks
   d. To stay up as late as they like
   e. To receive a 10-dollar allowance per week with no responsibility
   f. An all-expense-paid vacation to Disneyland for 1 week
   g. A 2-week, all-expense-paid vacation for your parents, wherever they want to go
   h. The opportunity to eat whatever you wanted for 6 months
   i. The opportunity to have no one tell you what to do for 6 months
   j. The opportunity to become president of the United States
   k. The opportunity to spend one day with your favorite movie or TV star
   l. A guarantee that you will never be sick
   m. The opportunity to have a perfect friend for all your life

VARIATION

Have the children make up their own auction list.

MY FAMILY CELEBRA-TIONS

SUGGESTED NUMBER: 4 or more

MATERIALS AND SUPPLIES

Paper and pencil for each child

PROCEDURE

1. Have the entire group formulate a list of family celebrations.
2. Then ask each child to list the holidays his or her family celebrates and how they are celebrated.
3. Divide into groups of 4 or 5. Let the children discuss some of their family celebrations and the ways they observe these holidays.
4. Let each group plan a celebration for 2 of their favorite holidays.
5. Have each group report to the total group.
6. Ask the children to make some of these suggestions to their parents and then report back at the following meeting on their parents' reaction.

VARIATION

Let the class plan a holiday and then celebrate it.

GROUP STRATEGY

MATERIALS AND SUPPLIES

Two 3-by-5-inch cards for each group, one marked blue and the other green

PROCEDURE

1. The purpose of this game is to earn more points than the other team and to avoid hurting anyone's feelings.
2. Divide the children into 2 teams.
3. Space the teams so that they cannot hear each other's strategy.
4. This game is played in 9 innings, with the total score determining the winner.
5. Each team secretly selects a color.
6. When called upon, a member from each team brings forward his or her team's selection.
7. If both teams select blue, both teams receive 5 points. If both teams select green, both teams lose 5 points. If 1 team selects blue and the other green, the blue team receives a −10 and the green team receives +10.
8. After 9 innings, add up the points to determine the winner.
9. Discuss the following questions after the game:
   a. What was your group's strategy?
   b. How did your team choose a color?
   c. Did your team adhere to the purpose of the game?
   d. Did you trust the other team?
   e. Why did your team decide to change color? When?
   f. In order to win, did one purpose have to be emphasized over another?
   g. How did the team members treat the minorities on your team?

THAT'S HOW I FEEL ABOUT IT

SUGGESTED NUMBER: 1 or more

MATERIALS AND SUPPLIES: None

PROCEDURE

1. The leader poses a question to the group and allows the children to answer voluntarily.
2. Try to let as many students become involved as possible.
3. This simulation game gives the children an opportunity to explain their values and listen to the values of the others.
4. Do not spend more than 10 to 15 minutes on this exercise.
5. Suggested questions:
   a. What is your favorite food?
   b. Do you ever cook?
   c. What present would you like to give your best friend?
   d. How do you know when something is right or wrong?
   e. If you could change one thing about your life, what would it be?
   f. Are you proud to be a girl(boy)?
   g. Would you tell your best friend he or she has bad breath?
   h. Do you feel your teacher is fair?
   i. What would you do if you received too much change after purchasing an item from a store?
   j. Have you ever cheated at a game? Why? How did you feel about it?
   k. Why do you think your friends like you?

MONEY AND TIME MANAGE- MENT

SUGGESTED NUMBER: 3 or more

MATERIALS AND SUPPLIES

1. List of "Things to Learn" (see below)
2. Pencil and paper for each group

PROCEDURE

1. Divide the children into small groups, preferably 3 children per group.
2. Give each group a list of "Things to Learn" or write the list on the blackboard.
3. The main purpose of this simulation game is for each group to buy as many hours as possible with their 100 coins. They may not exceed 100 hours.
4. This is a good exercise for time and money management.
5. Suggested "Things to Learn" list:

a.	How to mow the lawn	20 coins	20 hours
b.	How to baby-sit	5 coins	10 hours
c.	How to get a job	30 coins	5 hours
d.	How to help your mother	30 coins	10 hours
e.	How to study better	25 coins	25 hours
f.	How to ride a bicycle	10 coins	20 hours
g.	How to play soccer	15 coins	15 hours
h.	How to improve your grammar	10 coins	20 hours
i.	How to be a better swimmer	30 coins	10 hours
j.	How to be more popular	30 coins	10 hours
k.	How to play checkers	15 coins	10 hours
l.	How to make friends	10 coins	5 hours
m.	How to build a model	20 coins	15 hours
n.	How to train your dog	15 coins	20 hours
o.	How to roller skate	5 coins	5 hours

MY NAME

MATERIALS AND SUPPLIES

1. Construction paper
2. Scissors
3. Glue
4. Old magazines
5. Crayons or pencils

PROCEDURE

1. Have each student create a banner from construction paper.
2. Each person prints his or her name vertically down the left side of the paper in large letters.
3. Have each child cut out magazine pictures that correspond to each of the letters in his or her name.
4. Glue the pictures next to the corresponding letters.

HOW I SEE ME AND YOU

SUGGESTED NUMBER: 3 or more

MATERIALS AND SUPPLIES

A list of selected terms for each group

PROCEDURE

1. Divide into groups of 3 to 6 and give each group a copy of the above list.
2. All participants are to share with the group how they see themselves and how they see each member of the group in relation to the selected term.
3. After covering all the terms or topics, ask the children to tell what term they like best about themselves.
4. Suggested terms:
   a. color
   b. cartoon character
   c. season
   d. flower
   e. game
   f. animal
   g. country
   h. food
   i. profession

VARIATION

Ask the children to explain their answers.

DETERMINA-
TION

SUGGESTED NUMBER: 2 or more

MATERIALS AND SUPPLIES

Chalkboard and chalk

PROCEDURE

1. On the blackboard, list some negative types of behavior that a child could experience, for example, stealing candy, not attending school, swearing, talking back to parents, not doing chores, fighting, lying, and so on.
2. The children rank the items, starting with the most reprehensible act and proceeding to the least objectionable act.
3. After each child has ranked the items alone, the group makes a determination.

YOUR SPARE TIME

The next 7 activities can be used as simulations in the following ways: (1) Acting out the situation; (2) make up a story and change the ending; (3) read the children the situation and discuss the questions. Change the situations and add more specifics to stimulate the children's interests.

SITUATION

1. This simulation game gives the children a chance to discuss how they would like to spend their spare time.
2. Every day after school each child has 3 hours to spend as he or she wishes.
3. Some suggested ways to spend spare time and the amount of time an activity takes:
   a. Play ball 2 hours and 1 hour free time
   b. Watch TV 1 hour; study 1 hour; play with toys 1 hour
   c. Play with a friend 2 hours and watch TV 1 hour
   d. Deliver papers all 3 hours
   e. School club 2 hours; TV 1 hour
   f. Craft class 2 hours; free time 1 hour
   g. Collect for Red Cross 1 hour; study 1 hour; watch TV 1 hour
   h. Play with a friend 1 hour; study 2 hours

DISCUSSION

1. Divide into small groups of 3 to 5.
2. Let each child decide how he or she would like to spend the 3 hours.
3. Let each person tell why he or she made those choices.

WHAT DID I LEARN?

SITUATION

Each child completes the sentences telling what he or she has learned that day.

DISCUSSION

1. Have each child write down his or her answers. If the children wish, they may discuss their answers.
2. Suggested sentences to be completed:
   a. I learned that I . . .
   b. I felt good when . . .
   c. I was upset when . . .
   d. I discovered that . . .
   e. I found that I . . .
   f. I was proud that I . . .

VARIATION

Have each child take one thing he or she has learned and work on it during the week (self-contract idea).

A TWO-WEEK CRUISE

SITUATION

1. The purpose of this simulation is for children to become aware of some of the values of a friendship.
2. You have won a 2-week cruise on a ship.
3. You are given a list with a description of the other children your age.
4. You and 4 other children will room together, eat together, and be a group for all activities during the 2 weeks.

DISCUSSION

1. Have each child select 4 other children with whom he or she would like to go on the 2-week cruise.
2. Divide into groups of 4 or 5.
3. Each group is to select 4 other children with whom they want to go on their 2-week cruise. All the children in the group must agree on the final choices.
4. Have the groups explain why they have chosen their particular four traveling companions.
5. Possible traveling companions:
   a. **Matt Richie.** Matt is very rich and knows it. He is very spoiled because he always gets everything he wants. His parents will give him a lot of money to bring on the trip, and he will buy things like ice cream, candy, and other snacks for his group. He will also bring some of his expensive and fancy toys.
   b. **Betty Beautiful.** Betty is the most beautiful of all the children. She is very shy but always does what the group likes to do. Betty's group seldom appears to be in trouble because she is so cute and is not the kind of person who gets into trouble.

c. **Alan Athlete.** Alan is the best athlete of the group. He is so talented that his group wins all the athletic contests. He is always telling everybody what to do and when to do it. If one member of the group is not very good at a certain sport, Alan will tell him; yet the team manages to win because of Alan.

d. **Tammy Truth.** Tammy will always tell the truth. She will never sneak anything or cheat at any of the games. If someone in the group does something wrong she will tell one of the adults.

e. **Freddy Friendly.** Freddy is friendly and nice to everyone. He is not very athletic and is small. He has a bad heart and cannot participate in many activities.

f. **Tommy Talent.** Tommy is very talented. He can play the guitar and sing. He tells a lot of jokes, and the group really enjoys his music. He is loud and many times gets the group in trouble because they stay up late at night laughing and singing.

g. **Heather Helper.** Heather always likes to help the group. She would do anything for the group. Everyone likes Heather. Sometimes in order to help the group, Heather tells small lies and is a little sneaky.

h. **Mitzi Moody.** Sometimes Mitzi is very happy and lots of fun. But at other times, Mitzi becomes unhappy and complains and is terrible to have around.

LET'S BUY A CANDY BAR

SITUATION

1. Five friends walk up to a candy machine.
2. The machine does not give change back and only takes the exact amount of purchase. There is no other way to obtain change except from your friends.
3. All candies cost 20 cents.
4. Friends and amounts of money:
   a. Matt has no money.
   b. Mitzi has a quarter and a nickel.
   c. Lisa has two dimes and two nickels.
   d. Christopher has three nickels.
   e. Emmy has two dimes.

DISCUSSION

1. Divide into groups of 5, if possible.
2. Have each group figure out how many candy bars can be bought.
3. What do the children do with the candy bars after they have purchased them?
4. What happens to the change that is left over, if any?
5. Have each group give a solution.

DEAR GABBY

SUGGESTED NUMBER: 5 or more

MATERIALS AND SUPPLIES

Pencil and paper for each child

PROCEDURE

1. The group is seated in a circle and instructed to write a letter to "Dear Gabby," describing a problem that either

they or a friend is experiencing. Or, the problem can be imaginary. These letters should be signed fictitiously.
2. The leader collects the letters and reads them aloud to the group.
3. The group plays the role of "Dear Gabby" and discusses various solutions to the problems.

WHAT FRIENDS MEAN TO ME

SUGGESTED NUMBER: 1 or more

MATERIALS AND SUPPLIES

Pencil and paper or completion list

PROCEDURE

1. Pass out a completion list, write the list on the blackboard, or read it aloud.
2. Give the children incomplete sentences about friendship and have them complete the sentences.
3. Suggested completion list:
   a. It makes me happy when my friends . . .
   b. I hope my friends . . .
   c. I hope my friends don't . . .
   d. I'm unhappy when my friends . . .
   e. I'm proud that my friends . . .
   f. When my friends tease me, I . . .
   g. I do listen to my friends . . .
   h. I do not listen to my friends . . .
   i. I wish my friends . . .
   j. They are my friends because . . .
4. Only do 3 or 4 of these sentences in 1 session and allow all children to share their answers if they wish.

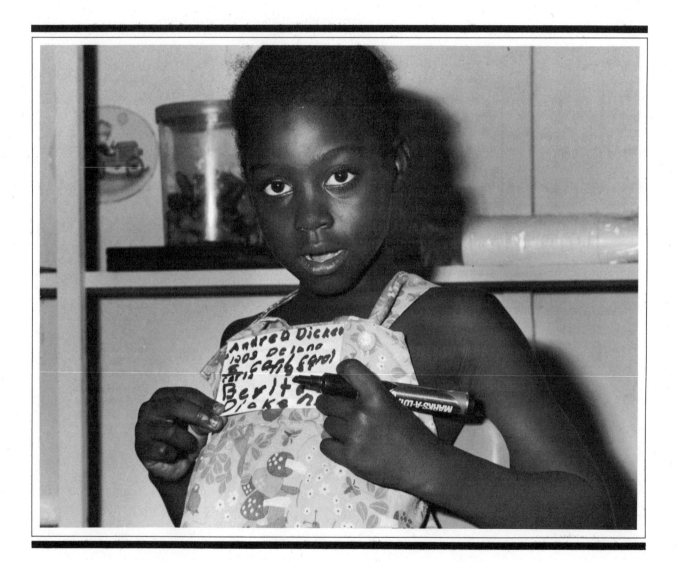

MAKING NAME TAGS

SUGGESTED NUMBER: 10 or more

MATERIALS AND SUPPLIES

1. Pencil for each child
2. A 5-by-7-inch index card for each child
3. Safety pin or straight pin for each child

PROCEDURE

1. Ask each participant to write his or her first name on the card so that it will be visible across the room.
2. The children are to write 5 words ending in "able" about themselves.
3. On the other side they again write their name.
4. Then they are to write 5 facts about themselves, for example, age, address, height, and so on.
5. Each child may then select which side of the card will be exposed and fastens the card to his or her clothing.

COOKING EXPERIENCES

3

MERINGUE STRAW-BERRIES

(serves 12)

INGREDIENTS

2 quarts of strawberries
4 tablespoons granulated sugar
4 egg whites
8 tablespoons confectioners' sugar
1 tablespoon vanilla flavoring

PROCEDURE

Have the children wash and stem the strawberries. Cut the strawberries in half and sprinkle with granulated sugar. Refrigerate until ready to use. Beat the egg whites until stiff, each child taking a turn with the egg beater. Gradually add the confectioners' sugar to the egg whites and continue beating until stiff peaks appear. Drain the juice off the strawberries and add the vanilla flavoring. Fold the berries into the egg whites. Spoon into chilled glasses and eat. This may be topped with whipped cream.

FRUIT PUNCH

(serves 10)

INGREDIENTS

20 strawberries
 5 bananas
10 tablespoons orange juice
10 teaspoons sugar
 5 cups milk

PROCEDURE

Have the children wash and stem the strawberries and peel the bananas. Then let the children take turns mashing the strawberries and bananas. Place all the ingredients in a closed jar and give each child 10 shakes to mix the fruit punch together. If all the ingredients will not fit into the jar, repeat the process until everyone is served.

SQUEEZED JUICES AND ZOMBIES

INGREDIENTS

Lemons
Oranges
Grapefruit

PROCEDURE

Have the children roll the fruit on the table so that more juice can be squeezed from the fruit.

If the children want to make lemonade, they must mix the juice from every half-lemon with ½ cup water and 2 teaspoons of sugar.

For orange juice, add ½ cup water for the juice from every half-orange.

Grapefruit juice is made by mixing ½ cup water with the juice from every half-grapefruit.

A Zombie is a drink that the children create with their own combinations of the above 3 juices. Allow each child to pour ½ cup of the juice of his or her choice into a pitcher. After everyone has poured a portion of the juice into the pitcher, it is ready to drink.

EGGNOG

INGREDIENTS

10 eggs
10 tablespoons sugar
1½ teaspoons vanilla
7½ cups milk
      nutmeg

PROCEDURE

Crack the eggs and give each child a chance to beat the eggs until foamy. Add the sugar and vanilla and beat until well mixed. Pour into glasses and sprinkle with nutmeg.

HONEY BUTTER

(serves 10)

INGREDIENTS

1 cup soft butter or margarine
¾ cup honey
    bread, Graham crackers, toast, or rolls

PROCEDURE

Have the children use an egg beater to whip the butter until it is creamed. Add the honey and beat until fluffy. Spread the honey butter on bread, Graham crackers, toast, or rolls.

AVOCADO DIP

(serves 10)

INGREDIENTS

3 ripe avocados
1 tablespoon mayonnaise
   dash of salt, pepper, and chili powder
   crackers, chips, or vegetables

PROCEDURE

Peel the avocados and have the children mash them with a fork. Add remaining ingredients and mix well. Use for a dip with the crackers, chips, or vegetables.

STRAW-BERRIES 'N SOUR CREAM

(serves 10)

INGREDIENTS

2 quarts of strawberries
1 8-ounce carton of sour cream
1 cup brown sugar

PROCEDURE

Have the children wash and stem the strawberries. The children can dip the strawberries into the sour cream and brown sugar and then pop the berries into their mouths.

APPLESAUCE

(serves 10)

INGREDIENTS

10 pippin apples
2½ cups water
¾ cup brown sugar
   cinnamon

PROCEDURE

Have the children peel, core, and slice the apples into small pieces. Place the apples, water, and brown sugar into a bowl and mix. Sprinkle with cinnamon to taste. Pour the ingredients into a hot frying pan. Have the children take turns stirring the apples until they are soft. This should take about 15 minutes. Have the children mash any whole apple that is left. After the applesauce has cooled, it will be ready to eat.

FRESH COCONUT

INGREDIENTS

1 fresh coconut with the outer green husk removed

PROCEDURE

The bottom of the coconut has 3 eyes. Hammer a nail through each of these and pull it out. Drain the liquid of the coconut out of these holes into a bowl (the children may drink the juice). To make the shell easier to crack, place the coconut in a 350-degree oven for 30 minutes. After the coconut cools a bit, wrap it in a towel and have the children take turns hitting it with a hammer. When the shell cracks, have the children pry off the white coconut meat with a knife. On one side of the coconut is a thin brown skin. Have the children peel it off with a vegetable peeler. The children can eat the coconut in tiny pieces for a snack, or they can put it in a food grinder or grater or blender for grated coconut. This can be sprinkled on desserts, whipped cream, cookies, and so on.

COCOA BANANA

(serves 10)

INGREDIENTS

10 bananas
2½ cups of confectioners' sugar
½ cup of cocoa
5 cups chopped nuts (walnuts, peanuts, pecans, or almonds)
2 4-ounce containers of whipped dessert topping

PROCEDURE

Combine the powdered sugar and cocoa and sift into a bowl. Place the nuts into a plastic bag, cover with a dish towel, and roll over the nuts with a rolling pin to chop them up. Have the children peel the bananas and cut them in half. Roll each banana half in the cocoa and sugar until it is covered. Place the bananas on a plate and pour the chopped nuts over them. Spread the cool whip on top of the banana halves. They are ready to eat.

SUBMARINE SANDWICH

(serves 6)

INGREDIENTS

    1 long loaf of sourdough French bread
 1½ pounds of mixed lunch meats, sliced thin
   ½ pound of cheese, sliced thin
    1 cup lettuce, shredded
    2 tomatoes
        mayonnaise
        mustard

PROCEDURE

Have the children shred the lettuce and slice the tomatoes. Slice the loaf of bread lengthwise through the middle but not all the way through. Carefully open the bread so that it lies flat; make sure the bread remains attached on the one side. Spread both sides of the bread with mustard and mayonnaise. Have each child layer lunchmeat, cheese, lettuce, and tomatoes on the bread. Mayonnaise can be spread between the layers of meat. Close the sandwich and use a knife to cut 2-inch wedges for each child.

HOBO SALAD

INGREDIENTS

        Fresh fruits (bananas, apples, pineapple, peaches, oranges, tangerines, cantelope, honeydew melon, strawberries, and so on)
   ½ cup honey
   ¼ cup lemon juice
   ¼ teaspoon salt
    3 tablespoons crushed pineapple

74

PROCEDURE

Have each child bring 1 piece of fruit from home to add to the salad. The children can wash, cut, peel, and slice the fruit. Put the honey, lemon juice, salt, and crushed pineapple in a closed jar, and let each child have 10 shakes to mix it completely. Pour the pineapple-honey dressing over the fruit, and the salad is ready to eat.

COLESLAW

(serves 10)

INGREDIENTS

5 cups shredded or chopped cabbage
¼ cup chopped onion (optional)
½ cup sour cream
¼ cup mayonnaise
½ teaspoon salt
½ teaspoon dry mustard
2 teaspoons lemon juice

PROCEDURE

Have the children chop or shred the cabbage and onion. Mix the sour cream, mayonnaise, salt, dry mustard, and lemon juice together and pour the mixture over the cabbage. Have the children take turns tossing the salad and then serve.

VARIATIONS

1. Omit the onion and add 2 cups diced tart apples.
2. Omit the onion and add 1 can (13 ounces) crushed pineapple, drained, and 1 cup miniature marshmallows.
3. Substitute 2 cups shredded red cabbage for 2 cups of the white cabbage.
4. Add grated carrots to the basic recipe.

POTATO SALAD

(serves 12)

INGREDIENTS

6 large potatoes (cooked with skins on)
4 sweet pickles
4 hard-boiled eggs
1 cup mayonnaise (or enough to moisten the potato salad)
  salt and pepper to taste

PROCEDURE

Have the children peel the potatoes. Then chop the potatoes, eggs, and sweet pickles. Add the salt, pepper, and mayonnaise and mix well. The salad is ready to eat or it may be chilled before eating.

COOL FRUIT-SHAKE

(serves 10)

INGREDIENTS

2½ cups powdered milk
3½ cups sweet fruit juice (apricot nectar or pineapple juice)
2½ cups chopped ice

Have the children put ice cubes into a plastic bag. Cover with a dish towel and crush the ice with a hammer. Put the ingredients into a large jar or plastic container with a lid. Have each child shake the container 10 times until the shake is mixed. Pour into glasses and drink.

YOGURT-CHEESE PUDDING

(serves 10)

INGREDIENTS

    5 3-ounce packages cream cheese
 2½ cups plain yogurt
    1 cup honey
    5 teaspoons vanilla flavoring

PROCEDURE

Have the children mash the softened cream cheese with a potato masher until smooth. Slowly add the yogurt, honey, and vanilla. Have the children continue mashing until the mixture is smooth. Allow the pudding to set a few minutes and then spoon it into cups.

CHEESE MODELING

INGREDIENTS

2 3-ounce packages of cream cheese
½ cup sour cream
1 package dried onion soup
good structure-building materials (bread sticks, pretzels, crackers, cheese curls, corn chips, rippled potato chips, and so on)
decorative materials (puffed flakes, cereals, popcorn, nuts, and so on)
Aerosol cans of cheese spreads (optional)

PROCEDURE

Mix the sour cream, onion soup mix, and softened cream cheese together to make the modeling compound. Each child must have a paper plate and knife to help with the construction. Flowers, bridges, tables, and cars are just some of the things children can construct by using the modeling compound to hold the building materials together.

HOMEMADE NOODLES

INGREDIENTS

2 eggs, beaten
½ teaspoon salt
1⅓ cups flour
extra flour in a bag
1 stick butter
1 can Parmesan cheese
1 tablespoon oil
water

In a large pot bring the water and the oil to a boil. Mix the eggs, salt, and flour together until well blended. Sprinkle flour on the table or on cutting boards. Have the children roll out the dough very thin with a rolling pin. Have the children use knives or pastry wheels to cut the noodles into ½-inch strips. Give each noodle a tug to stretch it. Drop the noodles into boiling water and cook 10 to 15 minutes or until tender. (A batch of noodle dough may be made up ahead of time so there will be enough noodles to eat.) Drain the noodles in a colander. Let the children serve themselves some noodles. They may put butter and cheese on the noodles before they eat them.

CARROT-RAISIN SALAD

(serves 10)

INGREDIENTS

- 5 cups grated carrots
- 1 cup raisins
- 1 cup mayonnaise (or enough to make mixture moist)
- ½ cup chopped celery
- salt to taste (celery salt may be used instead)

PROCEDURE

Have the children grate the carrots and chop the celery. Combine the carrots, celery, raisins, mayonnaise, and salt together, and the salad is ready to eat.

COLD CUTS AND CHEESE ROLLS AND STACKS

INGREDIENTS

ham
bologna
salami
American cheese
Swiss cheese
cream cheese
cheese spread

PROCEDURE

1. *Ham and Cheese Stacks*
   Have the children put a piece of ham on top of a slice of cheese and continue to stack the ham and cheese on top of each other until there are 6 layers. Cut the stack into squares and put a toothpick through each square.

2. *Bologna and Cheese Rolls*
   Have the children put a slice of cheese on top of a piece of bologna. Roll up the 2 slices and secure with a toothpick. A pickle can be added to the middle of the bologna and cheese roll.

3. *Salami Rollup*
   Have the children spread cream cheese or cheese spread on top of a piece of salami. Roll it up and secure with a toothpick.

CRESCENT CINNAMON ROLLS

INGREDIENTS

- 1 package of uncooked crescent rolls
- ½ cup butter or margarine
  large marshmallows
  cinnamon and sugar

PROCEDURE

Melt the butter in a saucepan. Have the children dip marshmallows into the melted butter and then roll them in a mixture of cinnamon and sugar. Place a sugar-coated marshmallow in the center of each crescent roll and pinch the edges closed. Dip the rolls in melted butter. Place in a muffin pan and bake as directed on the crescent roll package.

MOLASSES TAFFY

INGREDIENTS

- 2 tablespoons butter
- 1 cup molasses
- 2 cups non-instant powdered milk

PROCEDURE

Mix the powdered milk with the molasses and butter to form a stiff ball. Have the children stretch it until very stiff. If the mixture is too sticky, add more dry milk. Continue to stretch into a rope shape; then cut into pieces and wrap.

ICE CREAM

INGREDIENTS

1 ice bucket or plastic pail
1 egg
½ cup cream
1 teaspoon vanilla
  salt
  rock salt
  crushed salt

PROCEDURE

Beat the egg and honey in a coffee can. Add the milk, cream, vanilla, and a dash of salt. The can should not be more than half full. Cover the coffee can with the plastic lid. In the pail (or ice bucket) put a layer of ice and sprinkle with a spoonful of rock salt (table salt does not work as well but can be used). Place the coffee can in the pail over the layer of ice. Pack more salt and ice around the sides of the can up to the top of the can. Open the can and have the children take turns stirring the mixture with a big spoon. Allow the can to turn also. It will take 15 to 30 minutes for the ice cream to freeze to mush. It's ready to eat! If firmer ice cream is desired, put the can in the freezer for an hour.

HAPPY-FACE COOKIES

(makes 10)

INGREDIENTS

¾ cup confectioners' sugar
2 teaspoons milk
1 tablespoon peanut butter
  Graham crackers
  cinnamon candies, raisins, chocolate or butterscotch chips,
    coconut, or cookie decorations

PROCEDURE

Mix the confectioners' sugar, milk, and peanut butter together until spreadable. Have the children spread this on Graham crackers and create a face or other design on each cracker.

CHEESE STICKS

INGREDIENTS

1 cup sifted unbleached white flour
1 teaspoon baking powder
½ teaspoon paprika
½ teaspoon salt
1½ cups grated cheddar cheese
1 small egg, beaten
½ cup milk

PROCEDURE

Have the children grate the cheese. Then sift the flour, baking powder, salt, and paprika. Stir in the cheese. Combine the milk and egg and add to the flour and cheese mixture. Mix until the dough holds together; have the children roll it out on a floured board and cut it into strips. Place the strips on an ungreased cookie sheet and sprinkle with salt. Bake at 350 degrees for 15 to 20 minutes. These can also be cooked in an electric frying pan.

ENCHILADAS

INGREDIENTS

18 tortillas
½ pound Monterey Jack cheese
½ pound mild cheddar cheese
1 can pitted ripe olives
1 onion, chopped
2 tablespoons vinegar
 oil for frying
1 can enchilada sauce
½ cup water

PROCEDURE

Have the children take turns grating the cheese onto wax paper, cutting the olives into pieces, and chopping the onions. Place the cheeses, olives, vinegar, and onions in a bowl. Have an adult heat 1-inch of oil in a frying pan and in another frying pan heat the water and enchilada sauce. The adult dips 1 tortilla at a time into the oil until the tortilla is soft. Drain it on a paper towel, dip it in the sauce, and place it on a child's plate. Have each child fill a tortilla with the cheese mixture and roll it up and place it in a long pan or ovenproof dish. After all tortillas have been rolled up, pour the extra sauce over the enchiladas and cover with the rest of the cheese mixture. Place in a 350-degree oven and heat until the cheese melts. Dish up an enchilada for each child.

DRAMA AND STORYTELLING

4

MIME CREATIONS

SUGGESTED NUMBER: 1 or more

MATERIALS AND SUPPLIES: None

PROCEDURE

1. Have the children stand with enough room to move around freely.
2. Read a situation and allow the children 20 to 30 seconds to act it out, making full use of their bodies and using no words.
3. Suggested situations:
   a. washing dishes
   b. riding a bike
   c. peeling an onion
   d. opening a letter with good news
   e. vacuuming a rug
   f. directing traffic
   g. combing hair (hair remains tangled)
   h. hammering a nail (hit your thumb)
   i. make a baby stop crying

FACE PLAYS

SUGGESTED NUMBER: 4 or more

MATERIALS AND SUPPLIES: None

PROCEDURE

1. Divide into groups of 4 to 10.
2. Have each group develop a story (see From Words to Story, p. 90, or Finish a Fairy Tale, p. 90.
3. Each group then acts out the story for the other groups, without using words.

SKETCH-A-FRIEND

SUGGESTED NUMBER: 2 or more

MATERIALS AND SUPPLIES

1. Paper
2. Pencil, pen, crayon, chalk, or marking pen

PROCEDURE

1. Divide the children into pairs.
2. Have each child draw a picture or sketch of his or her partner.
3. Put the pictures up in the room and see if the classmates can identify them.

FROM WORDS TO STORY

SUGGESTED NUMBER: 4 or more

MATERIALS AND SUPPLIES: None

PROCEDURE

1. Have the entire group select any 5 unrelated words.
2. Divide into groups of 4 to 10.
3. Each group is to make up a story or play using the 5 words.
4. After a set time, have each group tell or act out its play.

FINISH A FAIRY TALE

SUGGESTED NUMBER: 4 or more

MATERIALS AND SUPPLIES

A book of fairy tales

PROCEDURE

1. Divide into groups of 4 to 10.
2. Read a fairy tale to the entire group, either finishing the tale or stopping at a key point.
3. Have the groups meet separately and finish or change the tale.
4. After a set time, have the groups return and act out the entire story, incorporating their endings.

STORY-GRAMS

SUGGESTED NUMBER: 1 or more

MATERIALS AND SUPPLIES

Pencil and paper for each child

PROCEDURE

1. The leader calls out 4, 5, or 6 letters, and the group makes up a sentence from the letters.
2. Each group must compose a sentence using words beginning with those letters and using the letters in the order they were given.
3. Do this 7 or 8 times until the group is able to make up a story from the sentences.
4. Have each group read its story.

MAD ADS

SUGGESTED NUMBER: 5 to 10

MATERIALS AND SUPPLIES

Paper and pencil

PROCEDURE

1. Use a familiar short story for this game such as the "Three Little Pigs."
2. Write out the story, leaving out a majority of verbs, adjectives, and nouns. The first few sentences might look like this: Once upon a time, there were _____ little _____. They left _____ to find their _____ and _____. One day they were _____ along the road.
3. Ask the children to put an appropriate word in each blank space. Tell them what type of word you are looking for (animal, number, action word).
4. When the children have filled in all the blanks, read the story to the class. It's guaranteed laughter.

STORY PULL

SUGGESTED NUMBER: 2 to 20

MATERIALS AND SUPPLIES

1. Paper
2. 5 paper bags

PROCEDURE

1. Write each of the following labels on a paper bag: Place, Person, Weather, Mood, Activity.
2. On slips of paper, write words that fall into each category. Here are some suggestions: Place—jungle, desert, mountains, Disneyland, circus; Person—old man, Easter Bunny, school teacher, dog catcher, sailor; Weather—rainy, sunny, windy, hot; Mood—happy, sad, grumpy, sleepy, angry; Activity—selling ice cream, flying a kite, catching butterflies, eating watermelon.
3. Each child must pull 1 slip of paper from each bag and then make up a short story using the words on all his or her slips of paper. It is possible to end up with a story about a grumpy Easter Bunny who is flying a kite in a hot jungle!
5. The story might also include how the bunny got to the hot jungle, why he is grumpy, and why he is flying a kite.

REVOLVING AUTHOR

SUGGESTED NUMBER: 10 to 20

MATERIALS AND SUPPLIES

Watch with a second hand

PROCEDURE

1. Seat the group in a circle.
2. One child must initiate a story (Once upon a time . . .). After he or she has talked for 15 seconds, the leader yells "next."
3. The next child must pick up the story for another 15 seconds.
4. The story grows and grows until everyone has had 2 or 3 turns.
5. The leader should end the story at an appropriate time.

EVOLUTION

SUGGESTED NUMBER: 5 to 15

MATERIALS AND SUPPLIES: None

PROCEDURE

1. Assign a simple action to each child. Suggestions: jumping in place; swinging one arm.

2. Instruct each child to make his or her action turn into (evolve into) something else. For example, jumping in place could turn into popcorn popping, and swinging one arm could turn into throwing a bowling ball.
3. Use your imagination. Encourage the children to use their imaginations!

PASS A POEM

SUGGESTED NUMBER: 10 to 20

MATERIALS AND SUPPLIES

Paper and pencils

PROCEDURE

1. Arrange the group in a circle.
2. The first child writes 1 line of poetry and folds the paper over so that the next person cannot see what has been written.
3. The first child whispers the last word of his or her sentence to the next person and passes the paper.
4. The second person must write a line of poetry to rhyme with the word just whispered to him or her.
5. This continues until the entire circle has added a line of poetry.
6. Read the poem aloud.

PIPE-CLEANER DRAMA

SUGGESTED NUMBER: 5 to 15

MATERIALS AND SUPPLIES

1. Pipe cleaners
2. Hat or bag

PROCEDURE

1. Give each child several pipe cleaners.
2. Instruct each child to make an object with the pipe cleaners that represents an activity he or she likes to do.
3. Put all the objects in a hat or bag.
4. Have each child reach into the hat and pull out one of the pipe-cleaner objects.
5. Each child is to interpret that object through pantomime.
6. See if the group can guess what activity the child is trying to dramatize.
7. It is fun to see how close each child's pantomime is to the intent of the object's creator.

WRITE A BOOK

SUGGESTED NUMBER: 5 to 15

MATERIALS AND SUPPLIES: Paper and pencil

PROCEDURE

1. Arrange the group in a circle.
2. The first child chooses a title for the book, writes it down, and folds the paper over. The title can be real or fictitious.
3. The second child writes the name of an author, folds the paper over, and hands it to the next child.
4. Continue around the circle, adding characters, chapter headings, plots, and finally the ending.
5. Be sure to fold the paper over every time so that the next child cannot see what has already been written.
6. When the book is completed, read it aloud to the class.

ACT IN A SACK

SUGGESTED NUMBER: 2 to 20

MATERIALS AND SUPPLIES

1. Large bag
2. Lots of small objects:
   erasers
   gum
   pencils
   dolls
   trucks
   sticks
   cups
   pictures

PROCEDURE

1. Put all the articles in a sack.
2. Arrange the group into pairs.
3. Have each couple reach in the sack and choose 5 articles.
4. Within 30 seconds the couple must create a story or skit that involves all 5 articles.
5. Each couple then presents their skit to the entire group.

HUMAN INSTRU- MENTS

SUGGESTED NUMBER: 5 or more

MATERIALS AND SUPPLIES: None

PROCEDURE

1. Have each child select a strange noise that can be made with the voice.
2. Let each child make this noise for the group.
3. Acting as the director, point to the noise you would like to hear.
4. Sounds may occur 2 or 3 at a time or all at once. You can experiment with the noises and create your own orchestra.
5. The children can take turns being the director.

PULL OUT A CHARAC-TER

MATERIALS AND SUPPLIES

1. Hat or sack
2. Paper and pencil

PROCEDURE

1. On slips of paper write down the names of characters and give them a personality trait that conflicts with their occupation. For example: a grouchy Santa Claus, a mail carrier who hates to walk, a lifeguard who is afraid of the water; a fisherman who hates fish.
2. Put all the slips of paper in a hat or a sack, and let each child pick one.
3. Give each child 30 seconds to act out with words and actions the type of character written on his or her slip of paper.
4. Encourage support within the group.

PHRASE IN A HAT

SUGGESTED NUMBER: 2 or more

MATERIALS AND SUPPLIES

Separate pieces of paper on which are written a complete or incomplete phrase for each participant

PROCEDURE

1. Have the children form a circle. Divide into 2 or more groups if there are more than 20 participants.
2. Fold each phrase in half and place in a container.
3. The first child draws out a phrase and begins a story. Then the second child draws a phrase and continues the story.
5. The story continues until every child has had a chance to draw a phrase from the hat.

VARIATION

If there are several groups, tape the story and play it for the other groups.

CHARADES

MATERIALS AND SUPPLIES

A watch with a second hand

PROCEDURE

1. One child is given a slip of paper on which is written a well-known quote or the title of a song, movie, TV show, or book.
2. Through actions only, the child acts out the subject word by word.
3. The group tries to guess the subject being acted out.
4. Before starting, agree on a series of signs such as categories, syllables, and so on.
5. Time each charade to see how long it takes the group to figure out the subject. Put a maximum time limit on each charade.

ONE-THOUGHT PLAY

SUGGESTED NUMBER: 4 or more

MATERIALS AND SUPPLIES: None

PROCEDURE

1. Divide into groups of 4 to 6.
2. Have each group select one thought.
   Suggestions:
   a. an empty car
   b. a scary night
   c. a lost boy running down the street
3. Make up a story from that thought.
4. Each group can tell the other groups the story or act the story out.

GROUP PROJECTS

5

CLAY MOBILE OR WIND CHIME

SUGGESTED NUMBER: 1 or more

MATERIALS AND SUPPLIES

1. Self-drying clay
2. Rolling pins
3. Nail
4. Knife
5. Embroidery hoop
6. Leaves
7. Fishing wire

PROCEDURE

1. Have the children take a walk to collect leaves.
2. Using a rolling pin, have each child flatten a lump of clay.
3. The children may use a knife to shape their piece of clay and a nail to make a hole in the top and the bottom of the clay.
4. Have the children place the leaves on the clay and roll over them again with the rolling pin. Remove the leaves and let the clay dry.
5. Paint the clay with tempera or acrylic paint.
6. Have the children tie a piece of fishing wire to the top of their clay piece and attach it to a friend's or to the embroidery hoop. The children must work together to get their mobile to balance. When every child has attached a piece, the mobile is ready to hang.

WEAVING MOSAIC

SUGGESTED NUMBER: 5 to 20

MATERIALS AND SUPPLIES

1. Small weaving-frames
2. Lots of yarn
3. Several large dowels
4. Fork

PROCEDURE

Frames

Materials: 10-by-18-inch pieces of ¼-inch plywood
1-inch finishing nails

Mark off ½-inch spaces on the top and bottom of the plywood and hammer a nail in each ½-inch mark.

Weaving

1. Run a piece of yarn from top to bottom of the frame by connecting it to each nail. This creates the warp.
2. Begin to weave through the warp with another piece of yarn. Be sure to go over and under every other strand.
3. When one row is completed, push it to the top with the fork.
4. Continue weaving until the warp is completed.
5. Finish the weaving by sewing the top and bottom so that the yarn won't unravel.
6. Remove the weaving from the frame.
7. Have each child complete 1 small weaving.
8. Loosely sew all the small weavings together to form a large weaving with a mosaic effect.
9. Attach the large weaving to the dowel and hang it in the classroom.

PAPER-PLATE CON-STRUCTION

SUGGESTED NUMBER: 1 or more

MATERIALS AND SUPPLIES

1. Round paper plates
2. Rubber bands
3. Pencil
4. Straight edge
5. Paper punch

PROCEDURE

1. Using the straight edge, draw an equilateral triangle on one of the paper plates.
2. Cut the triangle out and use it for a pattern.
3. Lay the pattern on a paper plate and trace the triangle. Put a notch at each triangle point by punching a partial hole with the paper punch.
4. Fold the 3 flaps toward the back of the paper plate.
5. To build a paper plate sculpture, take the flaps of 2 plates and put a rubber band around the flaps, making sure the rubber band hooks into the notches.

CARWASH

MATERIALS AND SUPPLIES

1. Soap
2. Water
3. Buckets
4. Rags
5. Towels
6. Cars

PROCEDURE

1. This project involves a wet mess, a lot of fun, and, one would hope, some clean cars.
2. Make a huge poster to hang in a conspicuous place outside your facility. Be sure to include the time and date and write "Free Carwash" in large letters. Also advertise that 25 or 50 or 100 dirty cars are needed.
3. At the appointed time, arrive armed with rags, towels, soap, and buckets.
4. Besides having the fun of splashing water, the group will learn to work together while initiating a feeling of community service.

COMMUNITY VEGETABLE GARDEN

SUGGESTED NUMBER: 2 or more

MATERIALS AND SUPPLIES

1. Seeds
2. Rakes
3. Trowels
4. Hose
5. Small garden area, large planter box, or pot

PROCEDURE

1. Have the group weed the garden area to prepare for planting.
2. Have the group decide what kind of vegetable to plant. Be sure to take into consideration the climate and time of year.
3. Prepare the ground for planting by breaking up the large dirt clods and raking it smooth.
4. Plant the seeds according to the directions on the package.
5. Be sure to take care of the vegetable seeds every time the group meets.
6. Harvest the vegetables as a group also.
7. Try making a stew or vegetable dish out of the harvest to eat together.

PATCHWORK MURAL

SUGGESTED NUMBER: 1 or more

MATERIALS AND SUPPLIES

1. Fabric remnants (children can bring them from home)
2. Rubber cement
3. Pinking shears
4. 1 square of material for each group's patchwork
5. 1 large piece of material to fit all the large squares

PROCEDURE

1. Divide the children into groups of 4.
2. Give each group a square on which to glue their patches of fabric remnants. With the pinking shears, cut 2-by-2-inch squares out of the remnants.
3. Have each group make a design with the squares, using the rubber cement to glue them on to the large square of material.
4. Have the groups come together and glue their squares to the largest piece of material.
5. When the patchwork mural is dry, it can be stapled to a bulletin board, framed, or used as a blanket or tablecloth.

TOPIC DRAWING

SUGGESTED NUMBER: 6 or more

MATERIALS AND SUPPLIES

1. Large sheets of butcher paper or drawing paper for each group
2. Crayons, pencils, paints, or other drawing tools

PROCEDURE

1. Divide into groups of 3 or 4 and pass out the supplies.
2. Give each group a topic about which to draw. There must be total group participation and each group must agree totally on the drawing.
3. After each group has finished, have them explain their drawing and allow other children to ask questions.
4. Suggested topics:
   a. invent the perfect toy
   b. the ideal backyard
   c. a person from another planet
   d. a new kind of animal, car, or TV
   e. a perfect classroom

POST OFFICE PUZZLE

SUGGESTED NUMBER: 5 or more

MATERIALS AND SUPPLIES

Any finished project, preferably one made by the group, that can be cut up

PROCEDURE

1. Cut a finished project into a puzzle and mail every person in the group a piece.
2. They are to bring their pieces of the puzzle to the next group meeting.
3. Put the puzzle together.
4. Emphasize group participation and the need for each individual to make the group whole.

MUSICAL MAGAZINES

SUGGESTED NUMBER: 5 or more

MATERIALS AND SUPPLIES

Numerous colorful magazines

PROCEDURE

1. Play a popular record with a message.
2. Seat the children around a table and ask them to cut out pictures from a magazine that best represent the song's message.
3. Each child then forms a collage and presents it to the rest of the children.
4. A giant collage can be made by attaching 4 or 5 of them together.

VARIATION

Take slides of the collages and the following week a slide presentation can be given while the song plays in the background.

DYE AND QUILT

SUGGESTED NUMBER: 5 to 20

MATERIALS AND SUPPLIES

1. Unbleached muslin
2. Several colors of dye (be sure the colors go together)
3. Rubber bands
4. Buckets
5. Curtain rods

PROCEDURE

1. Cut the muslin into 12-inch squares.
2. Give each child a square.
3. Distribute the rubber bands.
4. Form little puffs of material by twisting the rubber bands tightly around segments of the muslin square.
5. Mix the dye according to the directions on the package.
6. Dip each puff in a different color of dye.
7. Leave the material in the dye until it is a few shades darker than desired.
8. Only dip one color at a time, and be sure to dip the lighter colors first.
9. Wring out the excess dye thoroughly.
10. Remove the rubber bands when all the puffs of material have been dyed.
11. Allow the dyed squares to dry thoroughly.
12. Iron all the muslin squares.
13. Sew the squares together to form a patchwork design.
14. Hem the sides and mount on a curtain rod.

SHAPE AND BEND

MATERIALS AND SUPPLIES

1. Various colors of telephone wire
2. Large piece of flat styrofoam
3. Tin snips

PROCEDURE

1. Cut the telephone wire into large quantities of varied lengths.
2. Have the children sit within reach of the styrofoam and give each child several pieces of wire.
3. The wire will stand up when stuck into the styrofoam.
4. Sit back while the children bend and shape the wire into fantastic forms.
5. Soon the group will have a wire sculpture of a forest, a house, or a make-believe world.
6. Be sure to display with care.

NEWSPAPER COSTUMES

SUGGESTED NUMBER: 5 to 50

MATERIALS AND SUPPLIES

1. Newspapers
2. Masking tape

PROCEDURE

1. Divide into groups of 5 or 6.
2. Give each group a roll of tape and a huge pile of papers.
3. Have the children make costumes for every member of their group by folding, pleating, crumpling, and taping their newspapers.
4. Have the children create a skit around their costumes or make costumes for a specific skit.
5. Enjoy the costumes while they last—they are only good for 1 showing.

GIANT HAND MOBILE

SUGGESTED NUMBER: 10 to 20

MATERIALS AND SUPPLIES

1. Thick cardboard
2. Paint
3. Fishing line
4. Scissors
5. Pencils
6. Dowels (1 thick dowel and several thin ones)

PROCEDURE

1. Give each child 2 pieces of cardboard, each piece the size of a child's open hand.
2. Have the children trace their hands on the pieces of cardboard and then cut out the shapes and paint them in any way they like. Be sure to paint both sides.
3. When the cardboard hands are dry, punch a small hole in the top of each hand and attach a 10-inch piece of fishing line.
4. Give each child an 8-inch piece of thin dowel. Instruct the children to tie 1 cardboard hand to each end of the dowel.
5. Gather all the small dowels and attach them to the larger dowel. Instruct your group to work together to balance the mobile.

MAKE A CLOWN

SUGGESTED NUMBER: 2 to 20

MATERIALS AND SUPPLIES

1. Lots and lots of make-up
2. Mirrors
3. Cold cream
4. Tissues

1. Have each child find a partner.
2. Be sure the children have easy access to all the make-up they want.
3. Tell the children to design a clown face on their partners.
4. Stand back and watch a rainbow of clown faces appear.
5. If you must, the cold cream and tissues are for cleaning up.

CAN SCULPTURE

SUGGESTED NUMBER: 10 to 50

MATERIALS AND SUPPLIES

Lots of aluminum cans

PROCEDURE

1. Have the group collect as many aluminum cans as possible. You will need enough to cover 1 wall from floor to ceiling.
2. Choose a wall that isn't too big for the sculpture.
3. Stack all the cans on top of one another so that they fill the whole wall. Be sure the cans are all facing the same way.
4. Some interesting designs can be created by pulling some cans out farther than the others. Some suggestions: birthdays, child's name, holidays, holiday designs. Change designs as often as you like.

VARIATIONS

1. More-definite, 3-dimensional designs are possible by using smaller cans.
2. Turn some of the cans in the opposite direction to increase diversity.

PICTURE PUZZLE

SUGGESTED NUMBER: 10 to 20

MATERIALS AND SUPPLIES

1. Butcher paper
2. Paintbrushes

PROCEDURE

1. Give each child a 2-foot length of butcher paper.
2. Lay the butcher paper on the floor and ask the children to each paint a picture of himself on it.
3. When the painting is dry, cut it into several large puzzle pieces.
4. Mix up the pieces and see how long it takes the children to put the puzzle back together again.

VARIATIONS

1. To make the puzzle more permanent, mount the painting on a large piece of cardboard before cutting.
2. Use a photograph of the children for the puzzle.

GROUP MURALS

SUGGESTED NUMBER: 5 to 15

MATERIALS AND SUPPLIES

1. Butcher paper
2. Scrap paper
3. Crayons
4. Glue
5. Paint
6. Magazines

PROCEDURE

1. Give the children a theme for their mural. Suggestions: things that make me sad; things that make me happy; spring; summer; how I feel today.
2. Distribute all the materials.
3. Allow the children ample time to draw, cut, glue, and paint their feelings on a common piece of butcher paper.

SCRIBBLES

SUGGESTED NUMBER: 6 or more

MATERIALS AND SUPPLIES

Pencil and paper for each child

PROCEDURE

1. Each child is given a pencil and paper and is instructed to scribble a continuous line on the paper in any form he or she desires.
2. After each child has scribbled a line, the paper is passed to the person on his or her left.
3. After all papers have been passed, each child draws an original picture, making the scribble an integral part of the drawing.

SAND CASTING

SUGGESTED NUMBER: 2 to 20

MATERIALS AND SUPPLIES

1. Plaster of Paris
2. Wet sand
3. Large boxes
4. Popsicle sticks

PROCEDURE

1. Place the wet sand in the large boxes.
2. Let the children draw in the sand with their fingers and with popsicle sticks. Carve a variety of sand etchings about ¼ to ½ inch deep. Keep in mind that the drawings will be reversed when the sand casting is complete.
3. Mix the plaster of Paris according to package directions.
4. Carefully pour the liquid plaster of Paris over the sand designs.
5. Allow the plaster to dry completely and then remove the entire piece.
6. Dust off the extra sand, and the plaster creation is complete.

SEE-THROUGH CURTAINS

SUGGESTED NUMBER: 2 to 50

MATERIALS AND SUPPLIES

1. Lots of clear straws
2. Various colors of yarn
3. Large crewel needles
4. Round curtain rod

PROCEDURE

1. Cut the straws into 1-inch pieces.
2. Choose a window or door for the curtain. Cut each piece of yarn the length of the window or door, plus an additional 6 inches.
3. Thread the needle and knot the yarn and begin to thread the straw pieces.
4. Make enough strands to cover the window or door.
5. Tie the strands of yarn on the curtain rod and hang in the window or door.

FRIENDLY SKELETON

MATERIALS AND SUPPLIES

1. Butcher paper
2. Tempera paint and brushes
3. Scissors
4. Crayons

PROCEDURE

1. Divide the children into pairs.
2. Cut the butcher paper into strips long enough for a child to lie down on.
3. Have each child lie down on the butcher paper while his or her partner traces around the body with a crayon.
4. Paint the body shapes and cut them out.

BODY MÂCHÉ

SUGGESTED NUMBER: 2 to 10

MATERIALS AND SUPPLIES

1. Toilet paper
2. Newspaper
3. Tape
4. Chicken wire
5. Paints
6. Shellac
7. Papier-mâché (purchase the instant type at a hobby store)
8. Sandpaper

PROCEDURE

1. Divide the group into pairs.
2. Give each couple a roll of toilet paper, a stack of newspapers, some tape, and chicken wire.
3. Have each child measure his or her partner's body with the toilet paper. This should include length and circumference of arms, legs, head, torso, and neck.
4. After taking the measurement, each child must create a body sculpture out of newspapers and tape.
5. When all the parts of the body have been formed, tape them together to form a large floppy body.

6. To add strength to the body shapes, attach chicken wire over all parts of the newspaper. This should form a stiff model.
7. Tear more newspaper into strips 1 to 2 inches wide and about 12 inches long.
8. Mix the papier-mâché according to package directions.
9. Dip the strips of paper into the papier-mâché.
10. Have the children squeeze out any excess liquid between their fingers.
11. Drape these strips over the wire form in a crisscrossing fashion.
12. Cover the entire form with 2 or 3 layers.
13. Smooth down all the rough edges with extra papier-mâché.
14. Allow the form to dry for a week.
15. Smooth all rough areas with sandpaper.
16. Let each child paint and shellac his or her self-sculpture.

TAB CURTAINS

SUGGESTED NUMBER: 2 to 15

MATERIALS AND SUPPLIES

1. Tabs from aluminum cans
2. Round curtain rod

PROCEDURE

1. This project could take several months.
2. Have the group start collecting tabs long before you are ready to begin the project.
3. Select a doorway or window for the tab curtain. Be sure the curtain rod will fit this opening.
4. Have the children sit in small groups of 3 or 4. Give each group a large pile of tabs.
5. Hook one tab onto another by inserting the long end through the circle of the next tab.
6. Form the first link of a chain by carefully folding the tab over the ring.
7. Continue attaching tabs and rings until the desired length to cover the door or window is reached.
8. As the chains are completed, attach the last tab around the curtain rod.
9. Hang the curtain in the selected window or door when the rod is full.

VARIATION

Use these curtains for a room divider.

WINDOW MURALS

MATERIALS AND SUPPLIES

1. 1 cup Bon Ami
2. 1 cup alabustrine (glass paint—a whitening, available at most paint stores)
3. 1 cup dry tempera paint
4. Water
5. Cans
6. Paintbrushes

PROCEDURE

1. Mix the ingredients together to form a pastelike consistency.
2. Have the children paint a mural on the windows with the brushes.
3. This can be easily washed off with water.
4. Mix the colors separately.

PEAS-AND-TOOTHPICKS SCULPTURE

SUGGESTED NUMBER: 1 or more

MATERIALS AND SUPPLIES

1. Dried peas (soaked overnight)
2. Toothpicks

PROCEDURE

Have the children stick toothpicks in the peas to create a sculpture. The children can make their own sculptures and connect them together at the end or they may build together.

PAPER CLIP STRUCTURES

SUGGESTED NUMBER: 1 or more

MATERIALS AND SUPPLIES: Paper clips

PROCEDURE

1. Join the paper clips together to form a structure.
2. The following are some suggested ways to join paper clips together:
   a. Pull 1 end out.
   b. Twist 2 ends together.
   c. Make an eye or circle.
   d. Open the paper clip all the way and form a *W* with a loop in the center.

MAYPOLE

MATERIALS AND SUPPLIES

1. One 7-to-10-foot pole
2. 36 yards of ribbon
3. Thumbtacks
4. Tape
5. Tissue-paper flowers, crepe paper, or ribbon streamers
6. Christmas tree stand

PROCEDURE

1. Lay the pole on the ground. Tape or thumbtack tissue paper flowers on the top. If streamers are used, tape the bottoms of all the streamers around the pole. The tops of the streamers are above the pole. Cut out 12 3-yard pieces of ribbons and attach these like the streamers. These will be taped over the streamers. Bury the bottom of the pole in a hole in the ground. If this is to be used inside, mount the Maypole in a Christmas tree stand.
2. The Maypole is ready to use. The following steps can be used to create a pattern:
   a. *Single Wrap*
      Number the children from 1 to 4 going to the right. All children go to the right for 32 counts to their original position.

b. *Double Wrap*

Odds go to the left 32 counts, holding their ribbons up high. Evens go to the right and under the odds' ribbons. Unwrap for 32 counts back to position.

c. *Spider Web*

Odds take 1 step in and go down on 1 knee, holding the ribbon high. Evens go to the right and under odds, taking 16 counts to move to 4 people and 16 counts to return to original position.

d. *Cross*

Number 1's walk to pole in 8 counts with their left shoulder next to the pole, facing right. Number 2's go in and line up shoulder-to-shoulder with number 1's, then 3's and 4's. All should be lined up in 32 counts. All move together, taking half-steps and looking toward the pole for 16 counts. Return to the pole in 16 counts. Return to normal position, allowing 8 counts for 4's, 3's, 2's, and 1's.

CONVERSATION GAMES

6

MEMORY QUIZ

MATERIALS AND SUPPLIES

1. Pencil and paper
2. A large variety of objects

PROCEDURE

1. Depending on the number of players, divide into groups or remain as individuals.
2. Have everyone stand in a circle and place all the objects in the center of the circle. Let the players look at the objects for 30 seconds. If a large number of children are participating, each group may have to look at the objects at different times.
3. Have each individual write down as many objects as he or she can remember.
4. Then have the individuals within a group compile a list.
5. Finally, have the entire group come up with a list.

FOOT PHRASES

SUGGESTED NUMBER: 5 or more

MATERIALS AND SUPPLIES

1. 4-by-6-inch sheets of paper or tagboard
2. Masking tape or rubber bands

PROCEDURE

1. Choose a phrase and write each word on a separate piece of paper or tagboard. There should be a word for each child.
2. Instruct the children to sit on the floor. Attach a piece of paper to one foot of each child.
3. Tell the group the phrase or write it on a blackboard. The children are to correctly arrange the phrase with their feet.

YES–NO

SUGGESTED NUMBER: 10 or more

MATERIALS AND SUPPLIES

10 beans, buttons, or any other such item for each child.

PROCEDURE

1. Have the children walk around the room asking one another questions.
2. A person who says yes or no during the conversation must give the other person one of his or her objects.
3. After approximately 10 minutes, have everyone recount their objects to see how many they have remaining.

NOAH'S ARK

SUGGESTED NUMBER: 10 or more

MATERIALS AND SUPPLIES

1. 1 chair for each child
2. 1 blindfold for each child

PROCEDURE

1. Divide the children into pairs.

2. Give each pair a name, with the idea that they represent two of the animals that went into Noah's Ark. Select animals that make easily recognizable noises.
3. One partner from each pair leaves the room and is blindfolded and led back to the room.
4. The other child stands behind a chair and attracts his or her partner by making the sound of their animal.
5. The blindfolded partner, by listening for the sound of the animal, finds the chair and sits down.

WORD HUNT

SUGGESTED NUMBER: 4 or more

MATERIALS AND SUPPLIES: Words on card

PROCEDURE

1. Hide the cards with words written on them before the children arrive.
2. The children hunt for the cards.
3. When all cards are found, the children arrange them in order to form sentences.
4. Well-known quotations or phrases should be used.

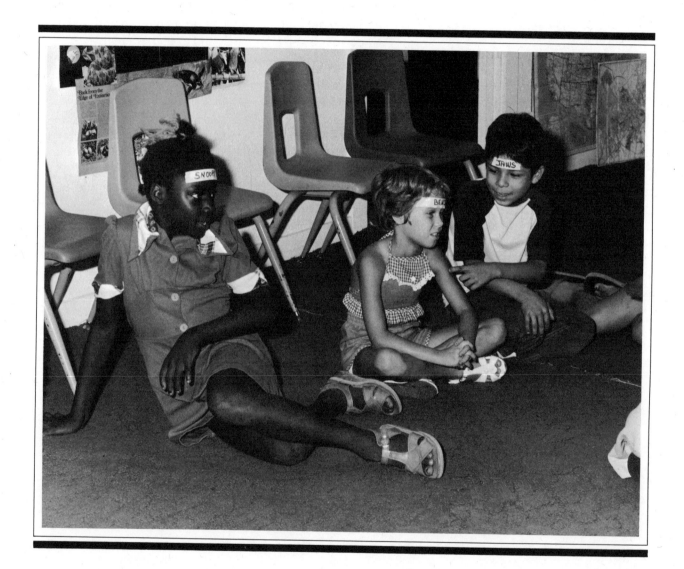

IT'S WRITTEN ALL OVER YOUR FACE

SUGGESTED NUMBER: 8 or more

MATERIALS AND SUPPLIES

1 roll of masking tape.

PROCEDURE

1. Before the group arrives, write famous names on the roll of masking tape and then tear off 1 name at a time. There should be 1 name tag for everyone in the group.
2. As the group arrives, tape a tag to each child's forehead. Each child guesses who he or she is by asking the other children questions.
3. Inform the group that all questions must be answered yes or no and that they cannot ask the same child 2 questions in a row.
4. The famous names should be ones easily recognizable to children, such as TV stars, rock singers, athletes, and so on.

QUIZ SQUARES

SUGGESTED NUMBER: 12 or more

MATERIALS AND SUPPLIES

1. A long list of questions and answers
2. 9 posters with X on 1 side and O on the other

PROCEDURE

1. This is a take-off on the TV show "Hollywood Squares."
2. A panel of 9 children is formed. Three sit on chairs, 3 stand behind, and 3 sit below the children in chairs.
3. Each child is equipped with *X's* and *O's.*
4. The rest of the children are formed into 2 groups and become the contestants. Assign one group to be *X's;* the other, *O's.*
5. The leader asks the *X* group to pick a square. The group decides who they want to answer the question.
6. The panel member questioned gives an answer, and the *X* group decides to agree or disagree. The leader gives the answer. If the group chose correctly, the panel member holds up an *X;* if they chose incorrectly, the panel member holds up an *O.*
7. The group alternates guesses as the game of tick-tack-toe becomes the object.

HAPPY BIRTHDAY GAME

SUGGESTED NUMBER: 10 or more

MATERIALS AND SUPPLIES: None

PROCEDURE

Have the entire group arrange themselves in one line according to their birthdate, youngest at one end and oldest at the opposite end.

NEWLY- FRIENDS

SUGGESTED NUMBER: 2 to 20

MATERIALS AND SUPPLIES: Paper and pencil

PROCEDURE

1. Arrange the children in pairs.
2. Give each couple five minutes to find out any information they can about their partner. Suggestions: shoe size; eye color; pets at home; how many brothers and sisters; age; favorite color.
3. After 5 minutes separate the couples, sending one out of the room.
4. Ask the remaining children questions about their partners and record their answers.
5. Have the partners return to the room.
6. Ask the returning partners the same questions and see if the answers match.

BODY SPELL

SUGGESTED NUMBER: 10 to 30

MATERIALS AND SUPPLIES: None

PROCEDURE

1. Divide the children into groups of 8 or 9.
2. Give the entire group 1 short word.
3. Each group must spell the word by using their bodies.
4. The children must be on the ground to get in the position of the letters.
5. The difficulty may be increased by using longer words.

THE NAME GAME

SUGGESTED NUMBER: 10 to 20

MATERIALS AND SUPPLIES

Name tags for every child

PROCEDURE

1. This game is best suited for a group of children who do not know one another.
2. Print a name tag for every child.
3. Attach someone else's name tag on each child. Be sure that it is in a visible place.
4. The children must find the person who is wearing their name tag. The children must also find the person whose name tag they are wearing.
5. Have the children switch name tags so that everyone is wearing the right one.
6. Ask the children to introduce the person whose name tag they first wore to the rest of the group.

SQUASH WALK

SUGGESTED NUMBER: Any multiple of 2

MATERIALS AND SUPPLIES: Playground ball

PROCEDURE

1. Divide the children into pairs.
2. Give each couple a ball.
3. Establish a goal for each couple to meet. Suggestions:
   a. Putting the ball in the wastebasket.
   b. Moving the ball across the yard.
4. Each couple must move the ball by placing the ball between their backs.
5. The children must try to walk while carrying the ball between their backs.

VARIATIONS

1. Put the ball between their chests.
2. Put the ball between their sides.
3. Use a ballon, water ballon, Ping-Pong ball, marble, or beanbag.

MIRROR MOVEMENTS

SUGGESTED NUMBER: Any multiple of two

MATERIALS AND SUPPLIES: None

PROCEDURE

1. Divide the group into pairs.

2. Have the children stand facing each other about 1 foot apart.
3. There should be an actor and a reactor for every pair.
4. One child initiates an action, and the partner follows the action with his or her own body.
5. The partners change roles so that each child has a turn to initiate the action.

THE STRING GAME

SUGGESTED NUMBER: 2 or more

MATERIALS AND SUPPLIES

A 3-foot piece of string for each player

PROCEDURE

1. Divide the children into pairs.
2. The leader ties one end of the string to a child's left wrist and the other end to the right wrist.
3. The leader takes a second piece of string, loops it through the tied person's arms and ties one end of the second piece to the partner's left wrist and the other to his or her right.
4. The two are now locked together. The object is to unlink without breaking or removing the string.

SOLUTION

The only possible solution is for one child to slide his or her string between his partner's wrist and string and then loop it around the partner's hand.

BLIND PAINTER

SUGGESTED NUMBER: 4 or more

MATERIALS AND SUPPLIES

1. Chalk and blackboard, paper and pencil, crayon and butcher paper
2. Blindfold

PROCEDURE

1. Divide the children into teams. Each team should have a maximum of 5 members.
2. Blindfold 1 member of each team.
3. The blind painter is to follow the instructions of team members as he or she paints the picture assigned to each team.
4. Each team tries to finish the drawing as quickly as possible. Have the entire group judge the drawings.

WORD PYRAMID

SUGGESTED NUMBER: 2 or more

MATERIALS AND SUPPLIES: Pencil and paper

PROCEDURE

1. If there are more than 2 players, divide the children into equal teams, with not more than 5 players each.
2. Give each team 6 letters that will spell a 6-letter word, 5-letter word, 4-letter word, 3-letter word, 2-letter word, *and* 1-letter word.

3. Example: S E T L A P
   A
   At
   Ate
   Late
   Slate
   Plates

MEET MY PARTNER

SUGGESTED NUMBER: 2 or more

MATERIALS AND SUPPLIES: None

PROCEDURE

1. Divide the children into pairs.
2. In 3 to 5 minutes, 1 child is to tell his or her partner as much as possible about himself or herself. The partners then reverse roles.
3. Now, ask each child to introduce his or her partner.

IN MY BAG

SUGGESTED NUMBER: 5 or more

MATERIALS AND SUPPLIES: None

PROCEDURE

1. Each child brings, in a paper sack, 3 or 4 items that describe something about himself or herself.
2. Ask each child to take out 1 item at a time and explain how that item describes himself or herself.

RIDDLES

SUGGESTED NUMBER: 20 or more

MATERIALS AND SUPPLIES: Numerous riddles and answers

PROCEDURE

1. Divide the children into 2 groups.
2. Give each child in one group a riddle; give the members of the second group the answers.
3. All children mingle and attempt to match the riddle to the answer.

FORM-A-LINE

SUGGESTED NUMBER: 10 or more

MATERIALS AND SUPPLIES: A measuring tape

PROCEDURE

1. Divide the children into 2 teams.
2. The object is to form a line in as many different ways as possible.
3. Possible events:
   a. Instruct the children to form the longest line possible by lying on the ground. One part of each person's body must be touching the person ahead of him or her.
   b. Form the shortest line possible by utilizing every member of the group.
   c. Form the tallest line by stacking the members of the group.

INSTRUCTO-RELAY

SUGGESTED NUMBER: 10 or more

MATERIALS AND SUPPLIES

A list of crazy instructions

PROCEDURE

1. Divide the children into 2 teams.
2. At a designated signal, a child from each team runs to a table across the room.
3. Each child takes a piece of paper that has an instruction written on it.
4. Each child runs back to his or her team and reads aloud the instruction. The team must then perform the task.
5. Suggested instructions:
   a. Take off your shoes, join hands and jump together 3 times.
   b. Sing "Jingle Bells" while hopping on 1 foot.
6. The game ends when each child has retrieved an instruction.

BUZZ ALONG

SUGGESTED NUMBER: 4 or more

MATERIALS AND SUPPLIES

Watch with a second hand

PROCEDURE

1. Divide the children into 2 teams.
2. Have each team sit or stand in a circle.
3. Each child on the first team takes a deep breath and begins to buzz.

4. Time the team to see how long it takes the last child to stop buzzing.
5. The second team then does the same stunt.

MATCH-AN-AD

SUGGESTED NUMBER: 20 or more

MATERIALS AND SUPPLIES

Numerous magazine advertisements, cut in half

PROCEDURE

1. Give each child one half of a magazine advertisement.
2. Instruct the children to find the holder of the matching half.
3. This game can be played with or without talking.

SHOE A PARTNER

SUGGESTED NUMBER: 20 or more

MATERIALS AND SUPPLIES: None

PROCEDURE

1. Divide the children into 2 groups.
2. Take a shoe from each child in one group and mix all the shoes together.
3. Each member of the second group grabs a shoe, finds its owner, and places the shoe on his or her foot.

HUMAN CHECKERS

SUGGESTED NUMBER: 16 to 24

MATERIALS AND SUPPLIES

24 pieces each of black and red construction paper

PROCEDURE

1. With the construction paper form a checkerboard on the floor.
2. All players begin in a leapfrog position.
3. Play regular checkers, except that each team must collectively agree on its move.
4. When someone becomes a king, he or she stands up.

FIND YOUR TEAM

SUGGESTED NUMBER: 20 or more

MATERIALS AND SUPPLIES: None

PROCEDURE

Have the children divide themselves into teams according to like characteristics.
Suggestions:
a. all children who have blue eyes
b. all children who have freckles
c. all children who have no freckles
d. all children who have a birthday between January and June

NEWSPAPER SHUFFLE

SUGGESTED NUMBER: 2 or more

MATERIALS AND SUPPLIES

A daily newspaper for each group

PROCEDURE

1. Divide into groups of 4 or 5.
2. Hand each group a daily newspaper with the pages out of sequence.
3. Each team is to put the paper back in correct order.

HUMAN CLOTHES-LINE

SUGGESTED NUMBER: 8 or more

MATERIALS AND SUPPLIES

1. A long piece of yarn or string
2. A timing device

PROCEDURE

1. Form the group into a circle.
2. Hand one child the yarn or string.
3. The lead child strings the yarn up his or her left sleeve through his or her shirt and pulls it out of his or her right sleeve. The lead child then passes it to the person on the right.
4. The game continues until all players are strung together.
5. This game can be played as a group effort against the clock or as a relay between 2 equal teams.

COMMUNITY FOOTHOLD

SUGGESTED NUMBER   Groups of 4

MATERIALS AND SUPPLIES

Pie pan for each group

PROCEDURE

1. Have the children lie on their backs with their feet in the air.
2. The heels of all 4 group members must be touching.
3. Balance the pie pan on the bottom of each group's feet.
4. Each group member is to take off his or her shoes one foot at a time while balancing the pie pan.
5. If children are of similar heights, the game will be much easier.